LET THEM COOK
BY JAYLON JONES II

Table of Contents

Author

Jaylon Jones II isn't your average 10-year-old. While most kids his age are playing video games, he's busy designing his own—and in between that, he's dominating the kitchen!

At just 5, Jaylon's love for baking was inspired by the sweet creations at Baby Cakes in Conroe, TX, and he's been mixing, whipping, and frosting his way to victory ever since.

With multiple 1st place and best overall wins in baking competitions, his skills are as sharp as his creativity. You'll find him kicking up a storm on the soccer field or basking in his music when he's not cooking delicious desserts.

Keep an eye out for Jaylon because he is just getting warmed up to help make your baking experience as easy and rewarding as his!

Chocolate Chip Cookie Cake

Prep Time: 10-15 minutes | Cook Time: 18- 20 minutes | Total Time: 28-35 minutes

Ingredients:

- ¾ cup unsalted butter softened
- 1 ½ cup dark brown sugar
- 2 large eggs
- 1 ½ cup chocolate chips
- 2 teaspoons pure vanilla extract
- 2 ¼ cups flour (all-purpose)
- ¾ teaspoon of salt
- 2 teaspoons of baking powder

Instructions:

1. Preheat oven to 350 degrees F.
2. Mix butter and sugar together until light and fluffy.
3. Add eggs and vanilla and stir to combine.
4. In a separate bowl, combine flour, salt, and baking powder.
5. Stir in the butter mixture until combined.
6. Slowly stir in chocolate chips.
7. Place dough into the center of a 12-inch (in) pie tin.
8. Spread the dough, leaving 1 inch of space btween the side of the tin and the dough.
9. Bake for 18-20 minutes.
10. Allow to cool before decorating.

Oreo Cake

Prep Time: 10-15 minutes | Cook Time: 7 minutes | Chill Time: 15 minutes | Total Time: 32-37 minutes

Ingredients:

Cake:

- 28 Oreo cookies
- 2 teaspoon baking powder
- 1 cup milk
- 6 in microwave-safe silicone cake mold
- 6 in parchment paper

Chocolate Ganache:

- 4 oz (1/2 a cup) heavy cream
- 2/3 cup chocolate chips

Instructions:

1. Crush the oreos in a large ziplock bag until the oreos become crumbs.
2. Put oreo crumbs in a mixing bowl.
3. Pour 1 cup of milk onto the crumbs.
4. Pour in 2 teaspoons of baking powder.
5. Mix until smooth.
6. Spray mold with cooking grease.
7. Place parchment paper inside of the mold.
8. Pour the mixture into the mold.
9. Microwave for 6 minutes in 60 second intervals.
10. Let stand in refrigerator for 15 minutes.

Making the Chocolate Ganache:

1. Pour heavy cream into a microwave-safe bowl.
2. Microwave the heavy cream for 45 sec to 1 min.
3. Stir chocolate chips into the heavy cream until smooth.
4. Pour over cooled cake.

Twinkie Pops

Prep Time: 10-15 minutes | Chill Time: 2 hours 15 minutes | Total Time: 2 hours 25 minutes-2 hours 30 minutes

Ingredients:

- Box of twinkies
- Melting chocolate
- Lollipop sticks
- Toppings (Sprinkles, Oreos, M&Ms, etc)

Instructions:

1. Unwrap Twinkies.
2. Put 1 lollipop stick into the bottom of each.
3. Freeze Twinkies for 2 hrs.
4. Melt chocolate based on package instructions.
5. Pour melting chocolate in cup for dipping.
6. Dip each Twinkie into the chocolate.
7. Let the excess chocolate drip off.
8. Place on wire rack.
9. Top with toppings.
10. Freeze for 15 minutes.

Cinnamon Rolls

Prep Time: 5-10 minutes | Cook Time: 8 minutes | Total Time: 13-18 minutes

Ingredients:

- 1 can of Pillsbury Cinnamon Rolls
- 1 can of cream cheese frosting
- Non stick cooking spray
- Tongs

Instructions:

1. Spray an air-fryer basket with nonstick cooking spray.
2. Place 4 cinnamon rolls 1 inch apart in the basket.
3. Air fry for 4 minutes at 350 degrees.
4. Use Tongs to turn cinnamon rolls over.
5. Air fry for an additional 4 minutes at 350 degrees.
6. Let cool, then frost.

Double Dutch Cookies

Prep Time: 10-15 minutes | Cook Time: 15-19 minutes | Chill Time: 15-20 minutes | Total Time: 40-54 minutes

Ingredients:

- 1 pack of ready to bake cookies
- 1 cup of chocolate chips
- Parchment paper
- 2 non stick baking sheets

Instructions:

1. Pre heat oven to 325 degrees.
2. Place cookies 2 inch apart on non stick cookie sheet.
3. Bake for 15-19 minutes.
4. Remove from oven.
5. Let cool for 15 minutes.
6. Line a baking sheet with parchment paper.
7. After the cookies cool, melt the chocolate chips in a heat-proof container.
8. Place your cookies, each at a go, into your melted chocolate. Pick the cookies up using two forks and place them on the baking sheet you prepared.
9. Let the cookies cool before serving.

Chocolate Fudge Recipe

Prep Time: 10-15 minutes | Cook Time: 1-5 minutes | Chill Time: 1 hour | Total Time: 1 hour 11 minutes-1 hour 20 minutes

Ingredients:

- 1 teaspoon of vanilla essence
- 2 cups of bittersweet chocolate chips
- 1 1/3 cups condensed milk

Instructions:

1. Line your pan, preferably 9x9, using parchment paper or foil and mist using the cooking spray.
2. Put the condensed milk and chocolate chips in a container, then combine.
3. Put the mixture in your microwave, heat/cook for a minute, then stir.
4. If your chocolate isn't smooth, put it in the microwave for one more minute or as needed.
5. Add in your vanilla essence and stir until combined.
6. Pour your now smooth chocolate into your lined pan, then refrigerate for 1 hour.
7. Cut into equal parts.

Cookies and Cream Ice Cream

Prep Time: 15-20 minutes | Chill Time: 24 hours | Total Time: 24 hours 15 minutes-24 hours 20 minutes

Ingredients:

- 2 cups heavy cream
- 1/4 teaspoon vanilla essence
- 1 1/3 cups of sweetened condensed milk
- 12 crushed Oreos
- 10 chopped soft chips ahoy

Instructions:

1. Crush oreos in a ziplock bag.
2. Crush soft chips-ahoy in another ziplock bag.
3. Add heavy cream to your bowl and whip until stiff peaks form.
4. Add sweetened condensed milk and vanilla extract.
5. Mix 1/2 of your oreos to your bowl.
6. Mix the crushed soft chips-ahoy into the bowl.
7. Transfer mixture to airtight container.
8. Top with the rest of oreos.
9. Freeze for 24 hrs.

Marshmallow Pops

Prep Time: 20-25 minutes | Cook Time: 1-5 minutes | Total Time: 21-30 minutes

Ingredients:

- 12 large marshmallows
- 6 oz melting chocolate wafers
- 12 lollipop sticks
- Toppings

Instructions:

1. Cover cookie sheet with wax paper.
2. Pour toppings into shallow bowl.
3. Insert 1 stick into the bottom center of each marshmallow.
4. Melt chocolate for 45 seconds and stir til smooth.
5. Dip 2/3 of each marshmallow into the chocolate.
6. Allow excess chocolate to drip off.
7. Sprinkle chocolate marshmallow with topping.
8. Place on wax paper to set/harden.

Chocolate mousse

Prep Time: 5-10 minutes | Chill Time: 3 hours | Total Time: 3 hours 5 minutes- 3 hours 10 minutes

Ingredients:

- 1/4 cup semi-sweet chocolate chips
- 1/2 cup plain yogurt

Instructions:

1. Melt chocolate for 30 seconds in microwave.
2. Once melted, add in the yogurt and mix together.
3. Pour the mixture into a small dessert dish and place in the fridge for 3 hours or until firm.

Galaxy Brownie Bites

Prep Time: 5-10 minutes | Cook Time: 1 minute | Chill Time: 5 minutes | Total Time: 11-16 minutes

Ingredients:

- 2 tablespoons cocoa powder
- 4 tablespoons flour
- 1 ½ tablespoons melted butter
- 3 tablespoons sugar
- 2 tablespoons milk
- 1 tablespoon Galaxy sprinkles
- 1 tablespoon mini chocolate chips

Instructions:

1. Put the flour in the microwave for 1 minute.
2. Let flour cool for at least 5 minutes.
3. Add all the ingredients to the bowl of flour and mix to form a cookie dough.
4. Add the sprinkles and chocolate chips and fold into the dough.

Ice cream sandwich

Prep Time: 5 minutes | Chill Time: 1 hour | Total Time: 1 hour 5 minutes

Ingredients:

- 2 pop tarts
- ½ cup cool whip

Instructions:

1. Spread the cool whip on the back of each pop tart and place on top of each other.
2. Freeze for 1 hour.

Red velvet oreo cookies

Prep Time: 10-15 minutes | Cook Time: 10-12 minutes | Total Time: 20-27 minutes

Ingredients:

- 1 box red velvet cake mix
- 5 tablespoon melted butter
- 2 eggs
- 4 chopped Oreos
- 1/2 cup white chocolate chips
- Cooking spray

Instructions:

1. Preheat the oven to 350ºF (180ºC).
2. Spray the baking sheet with cooking spray.
3. Add the cake mix, eggs, and melted butter to a bowl and mix to form a dough.
4. Fold the white chocolate chips and Oreos into the dough.
5. Form dough into 2 inch balls and add them to the baking sheet.
6. Bake the cookies for about 10-12 minutes.

Nutella fudge

Prep Time: 5 minutes | Cook Time: 2 minutes | Chill Time: 2 hours | Total Time: 2 hours 7 minutes

Ingredients:

- 2 1/3 cups chocolate chips
- 1 Cup Nutella

Instructions:

1. Add the chocolate chips and Nutella to a bowl.
2. Microwave in four 30-second increments (this means microwaving the mixture for 30 seconds at a time four times) until the chocolate melts. Stir after every 30 seconds.
3. Pour the mixture onto a baking sheet and refrigerate for 2 hrs.

White Chocolate Bark

Prep Time: 10 minutes | Cook Time: 2 minutes | Chill Time: 1 hour | Total Time: 1 hour 12 minutes

Ingredients:

- 1 ½ cups Golden Oreos crushed
- 2 cups white chocolate
- 1/8 cup rainbow sprinkles
- ½ cup mini marshmallows

Instructions:

1. Crush the oreos.
2. Add the white chocolate to a bowl and microwave in two 1-minute increments (for 2 minutes, 1 minute at a time), stirring between each one.
3. Add the golden Oreos, mini marshmallows, and sprinkles to the bowl and mix until everything is combined.
4. Pour the mixture onto a standard baking sheet.
5. Refrigerate for about 1 hour.

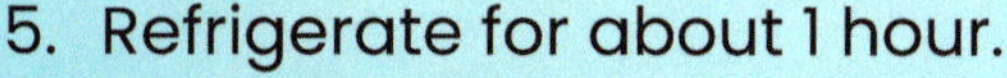

Nutter butter cake

Prep Time: 5-10 minutes | Cook Time: 24 minutes | Total Time: 29-34 minutes

Ingredients:

- 14 crushed Nutter Butters
- 1/2 cup milk
- 2 tsp baking powder

Instructions:

1. Preheat the oven to 340ºF.
2. Completely crush Nutter Butters in a ziplock bag.
3. Add the Nutter Butters, baking powder, and Nutter Butters to a container and mix to combine.
4. Put your mixture into a baking dish, preferably 4x4.
5. Bake for about 24 minutes.

Lemon Cookies

Prep Time: 15-20 minutes | Cook Time: 10 minutes | Chill Time: 10 minutes | Total Time: 35-40 minutes

Ingredients:

- 1 box of lemon cake mix
- ½ cup vegetable oil
- 1 box of pudding & pie filling
- 2 eggs
- powdered sugar

Instructions:

1. Mix together the cake mix, pudding & pie crust, oil, and eggs.
2. Refrigerate for 10 minutes.
3. Line the baking sheet with parchment paper.
4. Preheat oven to 350 degrees F.
5. Scoop the dough into balls.
6. Roll each ball in powdered sugar.
7. Bake for 10 minutes.
8. Cool for 10 minutes before serving.

Cupcakes 1/2 dozen

Ingredients:

- 1 cup of boxed cake mix
- 1/3 cup water
- 3 tablespoons vegetable oil
- 1 egg
- 1 cup frosting

Instructions:

1. Heat oven to 350 degree F.
2. Line 6 muffin cups with paper baking cups.
3. Mix 1 cup of cake mix with vegetable oil, water, and egg until smooth.
4. Divide evenly into muffin cups.
5. Bake for 20 minutes.
6. Cool for 10 minutes.
7. Frost as desired.

Simpson Donuts

Prep Time: 5-10 minutes | Cook Time: 2-5 minutes | Chill Time: 3 minutes | Total Time: 10-18 minutes

Ingredients:

- 1 pack of pillsbury butter biscuits
- 2 cups of strawberry frosting
- 2 tbsp milk
- rainbow sprinkles
- 1 cup vegetable oil

Instructions:

1. Cut out 1 in center of each biscuit.
2. Put strawberry frosting in a microwave-safe bowl with the 2 tablespoons of milk.
3. Microwave frosting for 30 seconds and set aside.
4. Heat cooking oil in Wok on medium heat for 1 minute.
5. Place biscuit into the oil and cook on each side for 30 seconds.
6. Remove from oil and place on wire rack.
7. Dip warm donut into the frosting and top with sprinkles.
8. Let cool for 3 minutes.

Hot cocoa bombs

Prep Time: 10-15 minutes | Cook Time: 2-3 minutes | Chill Time: 25 minutes | Total Time: 37-43 minutes

Ingredients:

- 6 teaspoons of small marshmallows
- 1 cup of milk chocolate chunks
- 6 teaspoons of hot cocoa powder

Instructions:

1. Melt your milk chocolate chunks using a microwave until smooth, stirring after each 30 seconds.
2. Scoop a tablespoon of your melted chocolate into your silicone cake molds (baking dishes), then spread the chocolate on the bottom and sides of your baking dishes using the back of you spoon.
3. Put your molds on a baking sheet, then freeze for 15 minutes.
4. Repeat steps 2 and 3.
5. Gently remove your half-sphere-shaped chocolates from your mold by peeling them back. Put the chocolates on parchment paper, then six of them with your marshmallows and hot cocoa powder.
6. Turn your stove on and set it to medium heat, then place your pan on it. Take the empty half-sphere-shaped chocolates, one after the other, and put them in the pan for around 3 seconds or til the rim melts.
7. Now, put the chocolates with melted rims on top of those filled with marshmallows and cocoa powder mix, then press until a tached.
8. Continue until you make six cocoa bombs.
9. Chill for 10 minutes.

Strawberry Brownies

Ingredients:

Brownies

• 1 box strawberry cake mix

• 2 eggs

• 1/3 cup of oil

Glaze

• 3 pureed strawberries

• 3 oz (3/8 cup) soft cream cheese

• 1 cup powdered sugar

Instructions:

1. Preheat oven 350 degree F.
2. Line pan with parchment paper.
3. Mix cake mix, oil, and eggs until smooth.
4. Bake for 20 minutes.
5. Cool for 15 minutes before adding glaze.

Making the Glaze

1. Mix strawberries, cream cheese, and powdered sugar until smooth.
2. Pour over the brownies.